I0439133

A Review of the Evidence on the Incidence of the Corporate Income Tax

by

William M. Gentry
Williams College

OTA Paper 101   December 2007

OTA Papers is an occasional series of reports on the research, models, and datasets developed to inform and improve Treasury's tax policy analysis. The papers are works in progress and subject to revision. Views and opinions expressed are those of the authors and do not necessarily represent official Treasury positions or policy. OTA Papers are distributed in order to document OTA analytic methods and data and invite discussion and suggestions for revision and improvement. Comments are welcome and should be directed to the author.

Office of Tax Analysis
US Department of the Treasury
1500 Pennsylvania Avenue, NW
Washington, DC 20220

The author is grateful to Deena Ackerman, Bob Carroll, Mike Devereux, Don Kiefer, Jay Mackie, and Jim Poterba for helpful comments. Comments are welcome; please direct them to William.M.Gentry@williams.edu. The author served as a consultant to the Office of Tax Analysis during the time this paper was written.

A Review of the Evidence on the Incidence of the Corporate Income Tax

Abstract

Who ultimately bears the burden of the corporate income tax plays an important role in the distributional analysis of tax policy. Distributional tables often assume that the incidence of the corporate income tax falls on the owners of capital but there is considerable uncertainty amongst economists about who bears the burden of the corporate income tax. This paper reviews the evidence on the incidence of the corporate income tax, especially in light of recent empirical studies that focus on the relationship between the corporate income tax and wages. While further research is necessary to draw definitive conclusions, these studies suggest that labor may bear a substantial burden from the corporate income tax. These empirical results are consistent with computable general equilibrium models based on an open economy in which a single country sets its tax policy independently of other countries; in these models, assumptions that capital is mobile and consumers are willing to substitute tradable goods produced in different countries imply that labor can bear more of the incidence of the corporate tax than capital bears. Evidence on the degree of capital mobility across countries and the sensitivity of corporate investment to changes in tax policy also corroborate the possibility that the corporate income tax lowers wages by reducing the productivity of the work force. In addition to changes in productivity associated with changes in capital intensity, labor may also bear part of the corporate income tax if wages are determined in a bargaining framework since the corporate income tax may change the equilibrium wage bargain. Overall, the recent empirical evidence, the open economy computable general equilibrium models of tax incidence, and the sensitivity of the amount of capital investment within a country suggest reconsidering the assumption that the corporate income tax falls on the owners of capital; labor may bear a substantial portion of the burden from the corporate income tax.

William M. Gentry
Department of Economics
Williams College
Williamstown, MA 01267
(413) 597-4257
William.M.Gentry@williams.edu

A Review of the Evidence on the Incidence of the Corporate Income Tax

I.   Introduction

Determining the incidence of the corporate income tax – that is, who actually bears the

burden of taxing corporate income – is of central importance in the debate over tax reform. The

corporate tax could be borne by some combination of the shareholders of corporations, investors

in all capital through a decrease in the overall return to capital, workers through a decrease in

wages, and customers through increased output prices. Depending on how this tax burden plays

out in equilibrium, the corporate tax can either increase or decrease the progressivity of the tax

system. Furthermore, given the possibility that the corporate income tax creates a variety of

distortions, the economic burden of the tax exceeds the amount of revenue raised by the tax; the

total distributional effect of the tax needs to account for this excess burden as well as the

revenues collected by the tax.

The actual burden of the corporate income tax depends on a complicated set of behavioral

reactions to the tax. The tax can change incentives for investment in the corporate sector, how

these investments are financed, and the location of investment across countries; in addition, the

corporate tax may favor some types of corporate investment over others. In turn, these

investment decisions can affect output prices by changing the cost of production and can affect

wages by altering how much capital firms use. Given the complicated nature of these changes, it

is not surprising that the incidence of the corporate income tax remains controversial among

economists. The complicated nature of these interactions has pushed applied research on

corporate tax incidence towards relying on general equilibrium models to inform the policy

debate. As discussed below, the conclusions from these models depend heavily on the

assumptions made in constructing the model. Until recently, empirical evidence on the incidence of the corporate income tax has been scarce. A nascent literature has developed that uses international data on corporate taxes and wages to estimate empirically the burden of the corporate income tax.

In this paper, I review this new empirical evidence on the corporate income tax. A common conclusion of these empirical studies is that labor seems to bear a substantial burden from the corporate income tax. This conclusion is in stark contrast to common assumptions used in distributional analyses of the US tax system that often allocate the corporate tax to the owners of capital.[1] As a way of determining the plausibility of these results, I examine the empirical evidence on the magnitudes of the critical responses in investment to changes in tax policy that must underpin the conclusion that labor bears the burden of the corporate income tax.

In addition to reviewing the empirical evidence, I place this evidence in the context of the general equilibrium models that have been the workhorses for predicting the incidence of the corporate income tax. These models have yielded a wide variety of conclusions about the incidence of the corporate income tax – ranging from capital bearing the burden of the corporate income tax to labor bearing the burden of the tax. One of the critical assumptions for these models is the choice between modeling a closed economy, so that capital does not flow between countries, and an open economy, in which international capital flows are central to determining the incidence of the corporate income tax. In the closed economy case, models often find that capital bears most or all of the corporate tax since the overall rate of return to capital falls as capital moves from the corporate to non-corporate sectors. Such models often assume that the effects of the corporate tax on the overall size of the capital stock are relatively modest since the

---

[1] Distributional analyses of the US tax system use a variety of assumptions about the incidence of the corporate income tax. See Barthold, Nunns, and Toder (1995) for a (somewhat dated) review of the assumptions used at various government agencies. While some reports include distributional tables that allocate a portion of the incidence of the corporate income tax to labor, the most common assumptions involve allocating the burden of the corporate tax (without adjusting for its excess burden) to owners of capital.

savings (and, hence, capital formation in a closed economy) does not respond strongly to the return to saving. In contrast, many open economy models predict that labor will bear the burden of the corporate tax under the assumption that capital is more mobile across countries than labor.

As Harberger (1995) points out, while the open economy assumption has considerable appeal as capital markets become more integrated, whether one should think in terms of the closed economy or open economy model also depends on whether all countries simultaneously change tax policy or a single country acts independently of other countries. If all countries simultaneously change their corporate income tax rates in a coordinated fashion, then the closed economy that focuses on the response of the total capital stock to the return to saving may be more appropriate than the open economy model that focuses on capital moving across borders. In contrast, if one wants to consider the effects of a single country changing its corporate tax rate holding other countries policies as fixed, then capital mobility across countries plays an important role in the analysis. Thus, the incidence of the corporate tax may depend heavily on the specifics of the proposed policy change and how other countries will respond to the policy change.

While general equilibrium models have been mainstays in analyzing the incidence of the corporate income tax, both Auerbach's (2006) recent review of the incidence of the corporate income tax and the empirical results of Arulampalam, Devereux, and Maffini (2007, discussed below) suggest that forces that are difficult to capture in such models may play an important role in determining who bears the tax. Specifically, Auerbach provides a number of reasons why shareholders may bear the burden of the tax without passing the tax to all capital owners, especially in the short term. One such mechanism is that the corporate tax falls, in part, on economic profits. However, Arulampalam, Devereux, and Maffini's empirical results focus on the possibility that wage bargaining provides a mechanism by which shareholders can shift some of the tax onto employees, even when a portion of the tax base is economic profit.

This review proceeds as follows. Section II reviews the recent empirical evidence on the effects of corporate income taxes on wages and the empirical challenges to measuring the incidence of the corporate income tax. Section III puts this evidence in the context of general equilibrium models and highlights behavioral responses that would be consistent with this evidence. Section IV discusses evidence on these various behavioral responses, including the responsiveness of corporate investment to tax policy and international capital mobility. The last section concludes with the implications of this evidence for setting corporate tax policy.

II. New Evidence on the Incidence of the Corporate Income Tax

A naïve view of the incidence of the corporate tax is that shareholders bear the burden of the tax through lower after-tax rates of return. This naïve view ignores the possibility that the tax will be shifted onto consumers through higher prices, workers through lower wages (possibly due to a fall in capital accumulation), or other types of capital as capital shifts out of the corporate sector in response to the lower after-tax return offered by corporations. To move beyond this naïve view, a model of economic behavior is necessary to guide predictions about how the burden of the corporate income tax will be distributed. Much of the literature on corporate tax incidence has focused on building such models and, depending on the assumptions, these models have generated a wide range of predictions.

Given the wide-range of possible burdens generated by taxing corporate income, the true incidence of the corporate income tax is an empirical question. Empirical work on this question faces a number of difficult challenges. First, at least if one focuses on a single country, there has been relatively little variation in corporate tax rates over time. While there has been more variation in tax rates across types of investment and across firms, such variation is problematic for testing general equilibrium tax effects since a part of this variation in tax rates is endogenous to firms' investment decisions. Second, a natural candidate for the dependent variable in a study of tax incidence is the rate of return to capital but disentangling the tax effects on rates of return from other determinants of rates of return (e.g., risk) is difficult. Separating the short-run tax incidence effects on rates of return, which might be captured more easily with data, from the long-run tax incidence effects, which are often the objects of theoretical models, further complicates empirical work on the effects of the corporate income tax on rates of return.

A trio of recent papers – Arulampalam, Devereux, and Maffini (2007); Hassett and Mathur (2006); and Felix (2007) – present new evidence on the incidence of the corporate income tax based on the relationship between cross-country variation in corporate taxation and wages. While corporate tax rates change infrequently within a single country, many countries have had major corporate tax reforms over the last 25 years. These papers exploit these tax reforms to measure the effects of corporate taxation. Instead of trying to measure how corporate taxes affect rates of return, these papers concentrate on whether corporate taxes reduce wages. By focusing on wages instead of rates of return to capital, these studies avoid some of the measurement issues associated with measuring rates of return as well as some of the short-run capitalization effects that can be conflated in estimating the effect of the corporate income tax on the rate of return to capital.

Despite many methodological differences across the studies (discussed in more detail below), the papers all conclude that labor bears a substantial burden of the corporate tax. Consider the following conclusions from the studies:

Our central estimate is that 61% of any additional [corporate] tax is passed on in lower wages in the short run and around 100% in the long run. (Arulampalam, Devereux, and Maffini, abstract)

Using cross-country panel data from the Luxembourg Income Study, I estimate that a ten percentage point increase in the corporate tax rate decreases annual gross wages by seven percent. Using U.S. data on corporate tax revenues and total wages, these estimates predict that labor's burden is more than four times the magnitude of the corporate tax revenue collected in the U.S. (Felix, p. 3)

The results in this paper suggest that corporate tax rates affect wage levels across countries. Higher corporate taxes lead to lower wages. A 1 percent *increase* in corporate tax rates is associated with nearly a 1 percent *drop* in wage rates. (Hassett and Mathur, p. 25)

Given the recentness of these papers, below I briefly review their results. Given the use of cross-country variation in tax rates used by these papers, they are mainly working in the spirit of open economy tax incidence: what happens within a country when it changes its tax policy without consideration of the tax policies of other countries?

II.A.   *Firm-level Estimates of Wage Effects*

Arulampalam, Devereux, and Maffini (henceforth, ADM) emphasize two potential channels for corporate taxes to affect employee compensation. First, the standard corporate tax incidence story that taxes affect firms' decisions about using capital and labor. The firm-specific changes in factor demands can affect wages even though workers have an outside wage option that does not necessarily depend on the corporate tax system. Second, to the extent that firms earn economic rents (in addition to just a competitive rate of return), workers and firms may engage in bargaining over these rents. The corporate tax liability can change the outcome of this bargaining.

ADM estimate the magnitude of this second effect of the corporate tax. Thus, their empirical approach does not capture the general equilibrium effects created by shifts in capital intensity. They use firm-level data on 15,433 firms from four European countries (France, Italy, Spain, and the UK) from the period 1993-2003. The dependent variable in their analysis is the logarithm of employee compensation per worker. They measure corporate tax burdens as the logarithm of the firm-level corporate tax liability per worker; this tax variable measures the amount of tax paid by the firm rather than a corporate tax rate. In addition to taxes, their empirical specification allows for compensation to depend on lagged compensation, value-added per worker, and year fixed effects. The inclusion of value-added per worker leads to their interpreting their results as arising from the bargaining channel; if the corporate tax leads to shifts in capital intensities, then these effects will be captured by the inclusion of the value-added per worker variable since changes in capital intensity will affect worker productivity and value-added per worker. The broader general equilibrium effects of the corporate tax would have additional effects on wages, returns to capital, and output prices.

Due to issues of endogeneity of the tax and value-added variables and persistence in the lagged dependent variable, ADM use several years of lagged data as instruments; the use of lagged variables as instruments reduces the useful time period over which they estimate their model to the last four years of the sample period. The ADM empirical model exploits variation in effective tax rates (i.e., tax liability relative to profit) across firms and over time. Since the effective tax rate is endogenous to profits and wages, they use lagged tax variables as well as country-specific measures of statutory tax rates and effective marginal and average tax rates as instruments. Thus, while they measure corporate taxes using corporate taxes per worker, they instrument for this tax measure using a variety of measures of the corporate tax rate.

Despite the challenges created by the persistence of firm-level wage data and the potential for endogeneity between taxes, profits, and wages, ADM find a statistically significant negative effect of corporate taxes on wages: a higher corporate tax liability reduces average worker compensation. In their baseline specification, they find a short-run elasticity of employee compensation with respect to corporate taxes per worker of -0.072. This elasticity is equivalent to a $1 in corporate tax liability reduces average compensation by $0.61 in the short run and around $1 in the long run. As an alternative specification, ADM replace the value-added per worker with the capital-labor ratio and a separate variable for the number of employees. In this specification, the corporate tax can have two effects on compensation: (1) the bargaining effect that is captured by the elasticity with respect to taxes per worker; and (2) an indirect effect by changing the capital-labor ratio. In this specification, the bargaining effect is about two-fifths smaller with an estimated elasticity of -0.042 (though only statistically significant at the 90% confidence level) and compensation is increasing in the capital-labor ratio with an elasticity of 0.220.[2]

As a test of whether bargaining could underlie this tax shifting result, ADM test whether firms that are part of a multinational group are able to shift more of the tax than purely domestic firms. The underlying hypothesis is that multinational operations may increase the firms' bargaining power. ADM find evidence consistent with this hypothesis: the elasticity of compensation with respect to corporate taxes is roughly twice as large for multinational firms as for purely domestic firms.

---

[2] To deduce the portion of the estimated effect of the capital-labor ratio on compensation that is due to taxes, one needs to know how responsive capital investment is to corporate taxation. Estimating precise relationships between taxes and investment typically requires substantially more data (in terms of variation in tax laws either over time or over place) than ADM have (see the investment studies discussed below). Nonetheless, ADM report results from a reduced-form specification that replaces the capital-labor ratio with the effective marginal tax rate. The effect of the effective marginal tax rate is negative (as expected) but quite imprecisely estimated and the elasticity of compensation with respect to taxes per employee falls to -0.027 and is not statistically significant.

II.B.   Effects on Household Wage Earnings

Felix (2007) approaches the question of the effect of corporate income taxes on annual labor earnings using quite different data than ADM. Her earnings data, taken from the Luxembourg Income Study, are from household surveys from 19 developed countries over the period 1979 – 2002.[3] For each year and country in her data, she measures annual labor earnings for low-, middle-, and high-skill workers (where education captures skill). Thus, she has three observations for each country-year in her data where the dependent variable is the logarithm of the annual gross wage for each skill-level. The main measure of the corporate tax rate is the top statutory tax rate; since this measure does not capture investment incentives such as depreciation allowances, the average tax rate (based on the experience of US multinational corporations operating in the country) provides an alternative measure of the extent of corporate income taxation. The empirical specification also includes the degree of openness of the economy (measured as the value of trade) and allows for an interaction between the effect of corporate taxes on labor earnings and how open the economy is.[4]

Felix's analysis yields three main results. First, the corporate income tax rate (measured either with the marginal tax rate or the average tax rate) has a negative effect on labor earnings. In specifications that do not interact the corporate tax rate with the openness of the economy, the estimated effect of a one percentage point increase in the corporate tax rate is a -0.50 to -0.70 percent decrease in annual gross wages (the range depends on what other control variables are included) but the estimated effects are not statistically significant. In specifications that include

---

[3] Data are not available for each country in each year. Given the data requirements for the study, it uses data from 65 country-year combinations.

[4] As control variables, the specification also includes workforce characteristics (education, age, and gender), personal income tax rates, GDP per capita, and random country-level effects.

interactions with the degree of openness, the estimated effect of a one percentage point increase in the corporate tax (evaluated at the mean level of openness) is a -0.71 to -1.23 percent decrease in the annual gross wage.[5] In discussing the magnitude of this effect, assuming that the effect of the tax rate on annual wages is -0.90 percent, Felix calculates that a one percentage point increase in the average US corporate tax rate would reduce aggregate wage earnings by roughly 4.2 times the additional corporate income tax revenue collected. While an effect of this magnitude seems quite large, it is consistent with the corporate tax creating considerable amounts of economic distortion in addition to the revenue collected.

Second, contrary to the hypothesis that highly-skilled labor will bear more of the corporate income tax than less-skilled labor due to complementarities between skill and capital, the negative effect of the corporate tax on earnings is quite uniform across skill groups. Thus, the model does not offer support to the possibility that the negative effects on wage income will accrue mainly to higher-wage workers.

Third, as expected, a greater degree of openness has a negative effect on earnings; however, the interaction term between the level of corporate taxes and openness generates somewhat puzzling results. A standard theoretical claim is that labor will bear more of the corporate tax in an open economy than a closed economy so one might expect a negative interaction between openness and the level of taxation. Felix estimates a positive coefficient on the interaction term when using the marginal tax rate and little relationship when using the average tax rate. Felix suggests that openness might also increase opportunities for corporate tax avoidance so that the corporate taxes are less important in more open economies, consistent with the estimated results.

---

[5] In specifications that use the average corporate tax rate instead of the marginal corporate tax rate, the estimated effect of a one percentage point increase in the corporate tax rate on the annual gross wage is -0.92 to -1.03 percent and statistically significant at the 99 percent confidence level.

II.C.   Effects on Manufacturing Wage Rates

Hassett and Mathur estimate the effect of corporate taxes using a broader sample of 72 countries with data from 1981-2002. Relative to the other two studies, Hassett and Mathur include a broader array of countries including many developing countries. Their dependent variable is the logarithm of the average hourly wage rate in manufacturing; they average their dependent variable over five-year windows and use dependent variables from the beginning of the window to explain variation in wages. As control variables, they include value added per worker in the manufacturing sector, the overall price level, the personal income tax rate, year fixed effects and country fixed effects. They use several alternative measures of the corporate tax rate: (1) the top corporate marginal tax rate; (2) effective marginal corporate tax rates; and (3) effective average corporate tax rates.

Across a wide variety of econometric specifications, Hassett and Mathur report a strong, negative effect of corporate taxes on wage rates but little effect of personal income taxes on wage rates. Thus, labor appears to bear a large portion of the corporate tax as well as the personal income tax on wage income. In specifications using the top corporate marginal tax rate, the elasticity of wage rates with respect to the corporate tax rate is roughly -1.0. In interpreting this result, Hassett and Mathur calculate that, setting all other variables to their average values, a one-standard deviation increase in corporate tax rates (i.e., an increase of ten percentage points from an average value of 35 percent) would reduce wages by 25 percent. This result seems exceptionally large. In alternative specifications using the effective marginal tax rate and the effective average tax rate, Hassett and Mathur reported estimated elasticities that are roughly half as large (and somewhat less statistically significant) as when they use the top corporate marginal tax rate. Thus, the magnitude of the effect is quite sensitive to how the tax rate is measured.

Given that ADM suggest that controlling for value added as a measure of productivity should make it difficult to estimate the effects of corporate taxes on wages that come through changes in capital intensity, one question about Hassett and Mathur's results is whether they are sensitive to controlling for value added. To address this issue, Hassett and Mathur estimate a two-step procedure in which corporate taxes can affect the capital-labor ratio (the first stage) and the capital-labor ratio can affect the wage rate (the second stage). While Hassett and Mathur find support for this two-step process in determining wage rates, they do not report estimates of the magnitude of the overall effect of corporate taxes on wages based on the estimated coefficients from this two-stage model.

Hassett and Mathur report two auxiliary results that suggest that international capital flows may play a substantial role in driving the results. First, in specifications that include wage rates and corporate tax rates in neighboring countries (defined either geographically or by income group), they estimate that both the wage rate and corporate tax rates of the neighboring countries have a positive effect on a country's wage rate. One explanation for this result is that a country (and its workers) benefit from higher capital investment when its neighbors have either high wage rates or high corporate taxes. Second, the estimated effects of the corporate tax rate are stronger for smaller countries, which one would expect are more vulnerable to the effects of being open economies.

Since Hassett and Mathur's original work, several authors have based other work on their approach. Felix (2007) uses her data to estimate a specification that is similar to Hassett and Mathur's main specification. Recall that her data focuses on developed countries and that the wage information comes from household surveys instead of being collected from manufacturing firms. Her data have few country-year observations but do calculate wage rates for different skill levels. Using the top corporate tax rate as her measure of the tax rate, she estimates statistically significant elasticities of the hourly wage rate with respect to the corporate tax rate that are roughly half as large as those reported by Hassett and Mathur.

Gravelle and Hungerford (2007) re-estimate the Hassett and Mathur specifications using alternative methods for adjusting wages for exchange rate differences. Hassett and Mathur convert wages for each country to US dollars using annual exchange rates; Gravelle and Hungerford point out that nominal exchange rates do not capture differences in the relative purchasing power within the two countries. Thus, they convert the wage variable to US dollars either with a Purchasing Power Parity (PPP) exchange rate or an inflation-adjusted PPP exchange rate. In specifications that use the top corporate tax rate as the dependent variable of interest, Gravelle and Hungerford report that these alternative exchange rate conversions reduce the estimated coefficient from -0.84 in Hassett and Mathur to -0.74 and -0.51, respectively, and the statistically significance falls to the 90% confidence level. Alternative measures for the tax rate lead to similar proportional declines in the estimated tax effects and the effects are no longer statistically significant.

II.D.   *Consensus and Challenges*

On the whole, this trio of studies paints a consistent empirical picture of corporate tax incidence: labor bears a large burden from the tax, possibly exceeding the revenues collected from the tax.[6] The exact magnitude of the estimated effect and whether these studies are robust

---

[6] In contrast to the consensus of these studies, an earlier empirical literature on the incidence of the corporate income tax failed to converge on a consensus. In the 1960s and early 1970s, several studies examined aggregate time series

to statistical challenges remains an open question. While all three papers use international data on corporate taxes and returns to labor and study a similar time period, their data sources and empirical methods differ substantially.

Despite the consensus among the papers, a skeptic might raise several general issues with the results. First, for the most part, the papers seem to be capturing corporate tax incidence over a relatively short-run horizon. If, as argued by ADM, the corporate tax affects bargaining over profits, then this wage bargaining might take several years before reaching equilibrium, depending on labor market institutions. If the effects of the corporate tax on wages come through changes in capital investment, one might expect that these effects would occur over several years.[7] Thus, the papers estimate short-run effects that one would expect to be smaller than the long-run effects. However, the timing might work in a somewhat opposite direction as well. Goolsbee (2003) estimates that, in the short-run, investment subsidies (e.g., changes in corporate tax policy to encourage investment) raise the price of capital goods and the wages of workers in capital goods sectors. Thus, a reduction in corporate tax burdens could increase wages of firms that supply capital goods to other corporations; however, since the suppliers of capital goods are also corporations, this effect could induce a negative correlation between wages and the corporate

---

data on rates of return and corporate taxes. Musgrave and Krzyzaniak (1963), Dusansky (1972), and Sebold (1979) find evidence of shifting (and possibly overshifting) of the corporate tax either onto consumers or workers; in contrast, Gordon (1967) and Oakland (1972) report that capital bears the short-run incidence of the corporate income tax. The contradictory nature of these results suggests caution in using long time-series data in estimating the effects of the corporate income tax. The lack of empirical consensus was one reason that computable general equilibrium models became the prevailing guides for analyzing the corporate income tax. Mulligan (2002, 2003, and 2004) revisits this approach using more recent empirical techniques based on Euler equations; his evidence is consistent with capital taxation being sshifted away from capital in the medium to long run.

[7] Presumably, the lag between changes in tax policy and the effect on the wage motivates Hassett and Mathur to examine the effect of the tax rate in a given year on average wages over the next five years. Gravelle and Hungerford (2007) report that Hassett and Mathur's results are sensitive to the choice of timing between the calculation of the wage variable and the tax rate variable. In a specification that uses the annual wage (using their real PPP-adjusted wage rate) instead of the five-year annual wage, Gravelle and Hungerford include the contemporaneous tax rate as well as the five years worth of lagged variables for the tax rate. While all of the estimated tax rate coefficients are negative, none of them are individually statistically significant. It is unclear whether the tax rate variables are jointly statistically significant or how important the choice of exchange rate adjustment is for comparing this specification with those of Hassett and Mathur.

tax. These wages changes could be transitory effects on wages so that the short-run relationship between wages and corporate taxes overstates the long-term effect.

Second, an important challenge for any empirical estimates of the response to taxes is to find exogenous changes in tax policy. To evaluate the long-term effects of policy, one needs data on permanent changes in policy and considerable amounts of data before and after these policy changes. Given the relatively modest time horizons in the papers and the relative infrequency of major corporate tax reforms, it is unclear whether the measured effects are capturing the long-run effects of tax policy.[8] Moreover, a common fear in econometric analysis is that the policy is endogenous to the variable of interest. For the relationship between wages and corporate taxes, this fear leads to the concern that governments shift towards higher capital taxation just before the returns to labor fall. Instead of the causality flowing from corporate taxes to wages, lower predicted wages induce higher capital taxation.

Third, the magnitudes of the results seem quite large based on *a priori* expectations about corporate tax incidence. In many specifications across the three papers, modest shifts in corporate tax policy lead to substantial changes in labor income. As will be discussed below, some theoretical models would support effects of the magnitudes reported but many parameterizations of theoretical models suggest the estimated effects are implausibly large. Nonetheless, the evidence suggests rethinking the common assumption that capital bears all of the corporate income tax seems warranted. Even if the true effect of how much of the corporate tax is borne by labor is smaller than most of the point estimates suggest, labor could bear a substantial burden from the corporate tax. The controversial nature of the results suggests that future empirical work building on these studies is necessary before drawing definitive

---

[8] Since ADM focus on firm-level variation in effective tax rates, their estimates are not susceptible to the criticism that tax policy is endogenous.

conclusions. Obviously, a sample of three studies is small for a meta-analysis of the issue; however, given the differences in approach across the three papers, it is intriguing that each paper finds large effects of the corporate tax on wages.

III. Theoretical Context for New Empirical Estimates of Corporate Tax Incidence

A natural question to ask is what theoretical model is consistent with the possibility that labor bears a substantial burden from the corporate income tax. This section proceeds in two parts. The first provides an overview of the results of a standard general equilibrium model; the second considers extensions to this model and other theoretical concerns.

III.A. Basic General Equilibrium Modeling Framework

Given the standard differences in the analysis of closed and open economies, the result is much more consistent with an open economy model. In an open economy, the corporate tax can cause a reallocation of capital across countries as well as across domestic sectors. If capital is mobile (and labor is immobile) across jurisdictions, then labor's share of the tax burden can be high.

A quantitative theoretical prediction for the allocation of the burden of corporate taxes requires building a specific model of the international economy. The task of building such a model is outside the scope of this review. Fortunately, recent papers by Randolph (2006), Harberger (2006), and Gravelle and Smetters (2006) carefully present general equilibrium analyses of the long-run impacts of the corporate income tax.[9] To fix ideas, consider Randolph's model of corporate tax incidence in an open economy. The model has two countries, each with

---

[9] The analyses in these papers build several earlier papers, including Bradford (1978), Harberger (1995), Melvin (1982), and Mutti and Grubert (1985).

five sectors and three factors of production (capital, labor and land). Of the five sectors, three sectors face the corporate tax: (1) a sector that produces tradable goods that are perfect substitutes with foreign goods; (2) a sector that produces tradable goods that are imperfect substitutes with the foreign goods; and (3) a non-tradable sector. The remaining two sectors are noncorporate with one producing tradable goods and the other producing non-tradable goods. All five sectors in both countries have production functions with constant returns to scale and markets are assumed to be perfectly competitive.

In general equilibrium models, predictions depend critically on assumptions about factor mobility and the variability of factor supplies. Randolph starts with the traditional assumption that capital is perfectly mobile across sectors within a country and across countries. Labor is mobile across sectors within a country but cannot move across jurisdictions. In the aggregate, capital is in fixed worldwide supply. Labor supply is in fixed supply within each country. These assumptions are critical since factor mobility, supply elasticities, and the relative capital intensities of different sectors drive the price changes that determine the burdens of the tax. One justification for assuming that factors are mobile is that the models are predicting the long-term effects of tax policy, rather than short-term effects.

Randolph focuses on a model in which the US has a corporate tax and the foreign country does not. One can interpret the results as the incidence of the difference between the US corporate income tax rate and the foreign corporate tax rate. Moreover, the predictions of the model apply to a change in US tax policy holding the tax regimes in other countries as fixed so the main results of the paper ignore the possible effects of tax competition among countries or other forms of interdependency between countries' corporate tax systems.[10] An alternative

---

[10] Randolph discusses the interaction between increased capital mobility and tax competition over the last 25 years. Below, I discuss the implications of tax competition for corporate tax incidence.

assumption about differences in corporate tax rates across countries is that both countries levy the same corporate tax rate; under this assumption, the assumption of a fixed worldwide capital stock pushes Randolph's model back towards the closed economy model in which capital bears the burden of the corporate income tax.

Under reasonable assumptions about factor shares and elasticities, Randolph's main results can be summarized as follows. First, domestic labor and capital bear the corporate tax roughly in proportion to their factor income shares in the economy; thus, labor bears roughly 73% of the corporate income tax (compared to receiving 70% of overall income) and capital bears 33% of the corporate income tax (compared to receiving 29% of overall income).[11] Second, the domestic corporate income tax has important implications for factor returns in the foreign country; a higher US corporate tax rate increases wages and decreases returns to capital in the foreign country. Expressed as a percent of US corporate tax revenues, foreign labor gains an amount that is equal to 71% of the corporate tax revenues and foreign capital losses an amount equal to 72% of the corporate tax revenues. These effects come from the increase in capital investment in the foreign country. With more capital, foreign workers are more productive but the return to capital in the foreign country falls.

In terms of domestic labor's share of the corporate tax burden, these theoretical results seem fairly consistent with ADM's results, despite ADM's suggestion that wage bargaining rather than changes in capital intensities underlies their results. In contrast, they are smaller than the estimated effects of Felix or Hassett and Mathur. In comparing these theoretical results with the empirical results discussed above, one needs to keep in mind that the corporate tax can affect

---

[11] The corporate tax burdens on domestic capital and labor do not sum to 100% for several reasons. First, these burdens are expressed as percentages of corporate tax revenues; since the tax creates a deadweight loss, total burdens exceed total revenues. Second, land is a third factor in the model; domestic landowners actually benefit slightly from the corporate income tax (land is primarily an input in noncorporate production). Third, as discussed below, some of the burden of the tax is borne by foreign factors of production.

real income both by changing the returns to factor (e.g., the wage rate) and by changing the overall price level. Randolph measures effects as the total effect on the sources and uses of income (i.e., the net effect of changes in factor prices and output prices). While a higher corporate tax rate reduces wages, it also reduces overall consumer prices.[12] In contrast, using a similar open economy, general equilibrium model, Harberger (1995) predicts that labor may bear a sources-side burden that is 2 to 2½ times the size of corporate tax revenues. In subsequent work, Harberger (2006) reports overall effects that suggest that domestic labor bears 96% of the overall (i.e., sources and uses effects included) burden of the corporate income tax. Thus, the isolated effect on wage rates may overstate the true economic burden on labor. How do the empirical studies handle this distinction? Felix does not control for the price level effects of the corporate tax and compares her results to Harberger's (1995) sources-side only model. Hassett and Mathur report that they obtain similar estimates regardless of whether they estimate a model of the nominal wage or the real wage. Since ADM use firm-level data, it is difficult for them to control for overall price level effects. Taken together, Randolph's theoretical conclusions seem to lend support to the overall impression from the empirical analyses that labor bears a substantial burden from the corporate income tax.

III.B.   *Extensions and Alternative Considerations*

Randolph's conclusions are quite consistent with the standard intuitions about corporate tax incidence in an open economy with competitive markets. A natural question to ask is how

---

[12] The effect on the price level in the model is a statement about relative prices across sectors. Randolph assumes that the first sector in the corporate sector is the numeraire good. The non-traded corporate good is relatively capital-intensive so its price increases relative to the numeraire good. However, the relative prices in the non-corporate sector (other than agriculture which is assumed to have a fixed world output price) fall due to a reduction in both wages and the cost of capital in the non-corporate sector.

these conclusions depend on the basic assumptions in the model. This section considers some of the major extensions of the general equilibrium model of tax incidence.

III.B.1. Imperfect Competition

Imperfect competition can come in many forms with a variety of implications for who bears the corporate income tax. In an important precursor to Randolph's work, Gravelle and Smetters (2006) highlight the importance of one particular form of imperfect competition: what happens to the basic open economy tax incidence prediction that domestic labor bears the corporate income tax when tradable goods are less than perfect substitutes across countries? As consumers are less willing to substitute between foreign and domestic goods, capital will become less responsive to tax differentials (even though there are no explicit restrictions on capital mobility). Firms will be able to raise output prices in response to an increase in capital taxation. Gravelle and Smetters conclude that "the open economy assumption does not automatically imply that domestic labor bears the long-run incidence of a corporate income tax even if capital is perfectly mobile (p. 4)." The incidence does not, however, automatically fall on domestic capital; instead, some of the burden may be exported to foreigners.

While Gravelle and Smetters raise an interesting caveat to the standard open economy result, several issues need to be addressed before dismissing the possibility that labor bears a substantial burden from corporate taxation. First, the degree of substitutability of domestic and foreign goods is an empirical question. Based on estimates from bilateral trade equations presented by Erkel-Rousse and Mirza (2002), Randolph concludes that the long-run demand elasticities are likely to be quite large so the case of perfect substitutes may be quite reasonable. Second, the Gravelle and Smetters collapses all corporate tradable goods into a single composite

20

commodity and applies an overall elasticity; as they discuss, alternative model specifications that allow for multiple corporate sectors with varying degrees of substitutability across countries and varying capital intensities complicate the analysis (see also Harberger, 1995, and Randolph). A more detailed model with multiple corporate sectors can reduce the effect of imperfect substitutability between domestic and foreign goods can imply that domestic labor bears more of the corporate income tax.

The imperfect competition that Gravelle and Smetters analyze is essentially a situation where each country has some market power, even though no firms have market power. Thus, they stay within the common general equilibrium modeling framework of perfectly competitive markets with constant returns to scale. This form of imperfect competition suggests that, even though capital can move across borders, capital will be less mobile than if foreign and domestic goods are perfect substitutes. Thus, Gravelle and Smetters argue that factors that influence the aggregate amount of capital (i.e., how saving responds to changes in the after-tax rate of return to capital) play a role in determining the incidence of the corporate tax even when capital is freely mobile across countries.

Of course, imperfect competition comes in many other forms, such as technologies that lead to oligopolistic industries or firms having control over scarce inputs (such as intangible capital). These forms of imperfect competition create challenges for general equilibrium modeling since the general equilibrium effects focus on the effects on the marginal rate of return but imperfect competition implies that some of the tax revenues come from taxing inframarginal sources of return. In his review of corporate tax incidence, Auerbach (2006) discusses the implications of these sorts of imperfect competition for corporate tax incidence. Not surprisingly, the implications depend on the specifics of what generates economic rent. Pure monopoly is a classic textbook case in which the portion of the corporate income tax that is a tax on pure monopoly profit cannot be shifted away from the owners of the monopoly. Other cases of imperfect competition provide much more ambiguous results.[13] A difficulty with drawing general conclusions about corporate tax incidence based on models of imperfect competition is that the degree of imperfection competition and the sources of deviations from perfect competition vary across industries in the economy.

The importance of considering the tax burden on economic rents increases when one considers the interaction between the tax system and firms' financing decisions. Typically, general equilibrium models consider the corporate tax as the difference between the tax rate on using capital in the corporate sector and the tax rate on using capital in the noncorporate sector. As emphasized by Stigliz (1973), to the extent that debt is the marginal source of financing for corporations and interest payments are tax deductible, the return to marginal investments by the corporation may not face the corporate tax.[14] However, inframarginal returns (e.g., from the returns to intangible capital that cannot be financed by borrowing) will still face the corporate tax and the usual general equilibrium mechanisms for shifting the corporate tax may not be relevant. On the whole, as summarized by Auerbach, a common sentiment is that the presence of economic rents combined with endogenous financing choices makes it more likely that capital (and especially shareholders of corporations as opposed to owners of all capital) bears the corporate tax.

---

[13] Davidson and Martin (1985) imbed a game-theoretic model of imperfect competition in a general equilibrium model of corporate tax incidence; depending on the relative capital intensity of the sector with imperfect competition, capital can bear more or less than 100% of a tax on capital even when capital is in fixed supply.

[14] Auerbach and Hassett (2003) examine the marginal source of finance for US corporations. For many companies, their results suggest that retained earnings and new equity are the marginal source of finance; however, they report considerable heterogeneity in the marginal source of finance.

The underpinnings of ADM's empirical work suggest an important caveat to this claim that shareholders cannot shift the corporate tax. They focus on the possibility that wages are determined through bargaining between the firm and workers. Thus, wages are not merely determined by the marginal product of labor, as is assumed by the general equilibrium models. By changing the amount of money over which firms and workers bargain, the corporate tax can affect the incomes of workers even if it does not change the amount of capital used by the firm or the output prices charged by the firm.

III.B.2. Labor Mobility

Randolph's open economy general equilibrium model makes the typical assumption that capital moves across borders but labor stays in the same location. Unsurprisingly, such a model results in the less mobile factor bearing the burden of interjurisdictional differences in taxation of the mobile factor. Naturally, as one increases the mobility of labor, one would expect that it becomes less likely that a tax on mobile capital will be shifted onto labor.

For the federal-level corporate tax in the U.S., this assumption seems quite natural since migration flows are relatively modest.[15] However, since the empirical evidence discussed above relies on a wide range of countries, the assumption of immobile labor may not be the best assumption with which to interpret their results. Specifically, Felix relies fairly heavily on differences in corporate tax rates across European countries, which tend to have more opportunities for cross-border migration than U.S. labor markets. Furthermore, recall that Hassett and Mathur find evidence that high corporate tax rates in neighboring countries are

---

[15] In contrast, if one were interested in the tax incidence of state-level taxes within the United States, assuming that labor is immobile would probably be unpalatable. Consistent with labor mobility affecting wages, Feldstein and Wrobel (1998) find that wages respond to interstate differences in taxation (albeit personal taxes rather than corporate taxes).

associated with higher wages in a country, consistent with mobility being the mediating force between tax rates and wages. Given the differences in labor mobility between the countries used in these studies and the U.S., it seems unlikely that a U.S.-specific result would suggest that labor bears less of the corporate tax than implied by the studies.

In addition to the possibility that labor moves in response to changes in factor prices, tax incidence can also depend on whether labor supply within a country varies due to changes in wage rates. The variation in labor supply could arise from changes in labor force participation decisions (including retirement decisions), hours worked conditional on being in the labor force, or changes in human capital (which can affect the effective amount of labor generated by a given number of hours worked).

III.B.3. Variable Factor Supply and Endogenous Savings

Randolph's general equilibrium model also follows the tradition of assuming fixed total factor supplies. Of course, the total amount of labor and capital can depend on tax policy. Allowing for variable factor supply (both labor and capital) moves us from what Kotlikoff and Summers (1987) refer to as static models of tax incidence, in which overall factor supplies are fixed, to dynamic models of tax incidence, in which factor supplies are endogenous. These models tend to focus on the long-run incidence of tax policy. However, as discussed by Auerbach (2006), these dynamic effects can affect tax incidence in the transition from one long-run equilibrium to another.

Fully accounting for endogenous labor supply and capital investment in a model of tax incidence is a daunting task since it requires specifying intertemporal choices of both savings and labor supply. One interaction to keep in mind is that the assumption of an open economy reduces the link between savings decisions and investment decisions within a country. With perfectly

mobile capital and perfect substitutability between foreign and domestic goods, the capital stock

and the eventual return to capital in a given country does not depend on the saving decisions of

the residents of that country. Capital mobility breaks the link between savings and investment

within a country.

If capital is less than fully mobile or other conditions conspire to keep capital from

flowing too readily in response to tax differences (e.g., Gravelle and Smetters' model of traded

goods being imperfect substitutes), then the savings response to differences in the rate of return

will affect the capital stock within a country. Savings within a country will partially determine

investment within the country. The magnitude of this savings response depends on households'

intertemporal elasticity of substitution. Unfortunately, economic theory does not make an

unambiguous prediction on the sign or magnitude of the relationship between saving and the

return to saving. Thus, the relationship between savings and the after-tax rate of return is an

empirical question.

Empirical work on the relationship between rates of return and saving has been

inconclusive.[16] One of the challenges for empirical work has been to identify exogenous

variation in the after-tax rate of return. For example, the level of savings and the return to saving

may be jointly determined by macroeconomic factors. Similarly, how a tax-induced change in

the after-tax rate of return affects savings may depend on whether the change in tax policy holds

overall fiscal policy (e.g., the government budget deficit) constant or not. In thinking about

corporate tax incidence, the natural starting point is what economists refer to as balanced-budget

tax incidence. Any change in tax revenue from altering the corporate tax rate would be offset by

other tax changes. This thought experiment eliminates effects on the capital stock that come

---

[16] For a survey of this research, see Bernheim (2002).

from government borrowing. Hence, the critical issue is the relationship between the rate of return and private saving.

To the extent that capital bears the burden of the corporate income tax, a higher corporate tax rate leads to a lower after-tax rate of return to capital. If private savings is positively related to the rate of return, then the savings response to a higher tax rate will lead to lower savings and lower domestic investment (taken as given that international capital flows are insufficient to eliminate the relationship between domestic saving and investment). The long-run implication for the incidence of the corporate income tax is that a higher tax rate leads to a lower domestic capital stock which leads to lower productivity and wages for workers. While there is uncertainty over the magnitude of these effects, it is unlikely that endogenous capital formation will reduce the burden of the corporate income tax borne by workers and it may substantially increase the burden on workers.

III.B.4. Tax Competition

The standard general equilibrium model of tax incidence assumes a tax rate differential between the corporate and non-corporate sectors within a country and, in the case of open economy models, a corporate tax rate differential between countries. The possibility of tax competition means that these tax rate differentials are not created in a policy vacuum. One country's tax policy can respond to the tax rates set by other countries. Tax competition raises the specter of a race to the bottom such that taxes on mobile factors cannot survive in an open economy.[17]

---

[17] For a comprehensive overview of international tax competition and its interactions with capital mobility, see Fuest, Huber and Mintz (2005).

Building a general equilibrium model that accounts for tax competition requires modeling how tax policy in one country responds to changes in tax policy in other countries. This naturally leads to considering strategic interactions among governments. If governments act in an uncoordinated fashion, one might conclude that capital income taxes will not survive in an open economy with relatively small countries (see, e.g., Gordon, 1992). The possible negative consequences of tax competition suggest that governments may want to foster institutions that will help coordinate tax policies across countries.

The policy implications of tax competition depend on whether a government thinks that its change in tax policy will induce other countries to change their tax policies. For example, a high-tax country reducing its tax rate to the average tax rate of other countries might engender a different response than a country with an average tax rate aggressively lowering its tax rate. For corporate tax incidence, the size of the tax policy response of other countries will determine whether capital actually flows across borders in response to a tax change. For example, if the US reduces its corporate tax rate and other countries do not change their tax rates, then the US is likely to attract more capital (so that labor will benefit from higher wages); in contrast, if the other countries respond to a US tax cut by cutting their tax rates, then the capital inflows might be relatively modest.

IV.   Corroborating Empirical Evidence

The empirical papers surveyed above suggest that labor bears a substantial burden from the corporate tax and this shifting may occur even in the short run. The general equilibrium models also suggest that labor can bear a considerable burden from corporate taxation. The extensions to the general equilibrium model considered in the previous section do not refute the

27

possibility that labor bears much of the corporate tax. Another way of addressing the validity of the empirical results described above is whether other empirical regularities are consistent with the observed relationship between corporate taxes and wages. In this section, I focus on the empirical evidence along three margins. First, how mobile is capital across countries? Specifically, is the location of capital sensitive to differences in tax rates across jurisdictions? Second, how sensitive is corporate investment to tax policy? Third, does capital migrate across organizational forms in response to tax differentials?

IV.A.   How Mobile is Capital across Countries?

Open economy models of tax incidence rely on the assumption that capital is mobile across countries so that investment in a country can respond to tax policy induced changes in the rate of return even if domestic savings does not respond. With mobile capital, capital can escape the burden of the tax. Two types of evidence are relevant for evaluating this assumption: (1) macroeconomic studies of the fluidity of capital markets; and (2) specific evidence on international capital flows in response to tax differentials.

The degree to which capital is mobile across countries remains a contentious issue in international economics. Part of this debate arises due to their being multiple definitions for "capital mobility" (see Frankel, 1992). On the one hand, capital mobility can be defined based on whether capital flows are strong enough to equalize real rates of return (controlling for exchange rate changes) from investing in different countries. Obstfeld's (1995) review of the capital mobility literature suggests that international capital markets work fairly well at eliminating arbitrage opportunities across financial markets in different developed economies. On the other hand, capital mobility can be measured based on relationships between domestic saving rates and investment rates. Feldstein and Horioka (1980) argue that high capital mobility should lead to a low correlation between saving and investment within a country; however, their empirical work suggests that the correlation is relatively high – a result that has been labeled the Feldstein-Horioka puzzle. Similar to the puzzle of high correlation between domestic saving and domestic investment, a number of papers have documented "home bias" in the portfolio investments of investors in different countries (see, e.g., French and Poterba, 1991, and Tesar and Werner, 1995).

The Feldstein-Horioka puzzle has generated extensive subsequent research, both in terms of econometric methods and challenges to the validity of the approach as a measure of capital mobility; Obstfeld (1996) provides a review of these issues through the mid-1990s. Furthermore, over the last 25 years, international capital markets may have become more integrated as countries have reduced capital controls (see Edwards, 1999). Several recent papers, including Blanchard and Giavazzi (2002) and Coakley, Fuertes, and Spagnolo (2004) argue that recent data suggests that the Feldstein-Horioka puzzle is disappearing, especially in the context of the European Union. Thus, the different measures of capital mobility may be converging on the conclusion that capital is mobile across countries.

Turning to the evidence on capital mobility responses to differences in tax policy, Desai, Foley, and Hines (2004) summarize the sizable literature on the responsiveness of foreign direct investment (FDI) to host country corporate tax rates as generating an elasticity of FDI with respect to after-tax returns of roughly -0.6; both time-series and cross-sectional econometric techniques produce similar estimates of this elasticity. Consistent with this consensus view, using a sample of US multinational firms, Desai, Foley and Hines estimate a similar elasticity of FDI with respect to the host country corporate tax rate; they also find that foreign affiliates' capital-labor intensities depend on the level of the corporate income tax in the host country.[18]

Moreover, other host country taxes (such as indirect taxes) also influence FDI. These tax effects arise despite the tax planning opportunities that US multinational firms can use to minimize their taxes without resorting to altering capital investment decisions.

While there is some controversy regarding the interpretation and continuing existence of the Feldstein-Horioka puzzle, in general, the evidence suggests that capital is quite mobile across countries. Covered interest parity tends to hold across countries suggesting little need for increased capital flows as a way of eliminating arbitrage opportunities. Corporate investment decisions appear quite sensitive to international differences in after-tax rates of return. Thus, the empirical evidence supports the open economy assumption for modeling the incidence of the corporate income tax.

IV.B.   How Strong is the Relationship between Investment and Corporate Taxation?

One channel through which the burden of a tax on capital can be shifted to labor is through changes in the amount of capital. Thus, in considering whether it is plausible that labor bears a substantial fraction of the burden of the corporate income tax, it is natural to ask whether capital taxation affects the level of capital investment. Fortunately, the relationship between capital taxation and investment has been studied extensively.

Hassett and Hubbard (2002) survey both the theoretical relationship between taxation and business investment and the existing empirical research. The basic theoretical model related investment to the tax-adjusted user cost of capital. This user cost of capital can depend on the

---

[18] While it is tempting to interpret the evidence on the responsiveness of US multinational's FDI to host country tax rates as evidence of a substitution of foreign investment for domestic investment, Desai, Foley, and Hines (2005) find that, for a sample of US multinational corporations, domestic and foreign investments are complements rather than substitutes. Thus, one should use caution in inferring that the sensitivity of FDI to foreign tax rates immediately translates into a reduction in the US capital stock and an increase in the foreign capital stock.

corporate tax rate but also depends on other aspects of tax policy, such as the generosity of depreciation allowances.

Through the mid-1990s, this empirical research could be characterized as suggesting that tax policy has relatively little effect on corporate investment. More generally, the early research on capital investment suggested that the entire neoclassical model of investment theory does not provide a compelling explanation of the data. The econometric problem has been to find exogenous variation in tax incentives for investment so that incentive effects can be separated from other influences on investment (e.g., the business cycle). More recent research, however, has overcome some of these econometric challenges and concludes that corporate investment is sensitive to tax policy. The empirical sensitivity of investment to the user cost of capital is typically measured as the estimated coefficient on Tobin's Q. Using data on U.S. corporations, Cummins, Hassett, and Hubbard reported estimated coefficients on Q of roughly 0.65. Other studies using U.S. data (see, e.g., Chirinko, Fazzari, and Meyer, 1999) report somewhat smaller sensitivities of investment to tax policy but their estimates are still statistically and economically different than zero.

Since the empirical studies of the effects of corporate taxes on wages focused on non-U.S. data, it is instructive to consider empirical studies on the relationship between tax policy and investment based on data from a similar set of countries. Cummins, Hassett, and Hubbard (1996) repeats the exercise of their early paper but uses data from 14 industrialized countries; the international data suggest a significant relationship between investment and tax policy in most countries, though the magnitude is typically (though not always) smaller than the estimated elasticity for the U.S. Using a sample of 85 countries, including both developed and developing countries, Djankov et al. (2007) examine the effect of corporate taxes on investment; rather than examine firm-level data using a user cost of capital model, they test whether investment-to-GDP ratios depend on the effective tax rate on investment. They report substantial negative effects of tax rates on investment rates: increasing the corporate tax rate by 10 percentage points leads to an investment rate that is 2.2 percentage points lower (compared to an average investment rate of 21.5%); much of the effect appears to come through a reduction in FDI.

Overall, a consensus seems to be emerging that investment responds to tax policy. The amount of capital in the corporate sector depends on the taxation of capital. This relationship is what one would expect to find if capital is able to move out of the corporate sector in response to tax policy and, as a result, labor may bear a sizable portion of the corporate tax.

IV.C.   Does Activity Shift between Corporate and Noncorporate Forms of Organization?

An alternative channel through which the corporate income tax can affect the amount of capital in the corporate sector is how capital is allocated across organizational forms. In the classic formulation of the Harberger model, the noncorporate sector produces different goods (e.g., housing) than the corporate sector. Reallocating capital across sectors meant changing the mix of outputs in the economy; this shift in output could affect the overall return to capital and labor. The substitutability of capital for labor in the two sectors will affect the eventual incidence of the corporate income tax.

In a pair of papers, Gravelle and Kotlikoff (1989 and 1993) build general equilibrium models in which corporate and noncorporate forms operate within the same industry. The corporate and noncorporate firms differ along one of two dimensions: (1) in the mutual production model, they differ in that corporate managers run corporations but entrepreneurs operate noncorporate firms and entrepreneurial skill is distributed throughout the economy; or (2) in the differentiated products model, the outputs of the types of firms are not perfect substitutes. In the first model, a tax on corporate capital can be good for entrepreneurs in the noncorporate sector since their talent becomes a more scarce resource; however, the gains of the entrepreneurs are not necessarily gains for workers in general and the model suggests that workers can lose from a corporate tax even when capital appears to bear 100% of the tax burden. With differentiated products across types of firms, the incidence depends on the degree to which consumers are willing to substitute goods and the relative elasticities of substitution of capital for labor in production.[19]

While these models illustrate the importance of considering endogenous organizational form from a theoretical perspective, one might also ask whether capital seems to be mobile across organizational forms. If so, then one would expect that this mobility would reduce the expected burden borne by capital from the corporate income tax. This mobility may suggest that the economic burdens of the corporate income tax exceed the revenues collected from the tax since moving capital to the noncorporate sector reduces tax revenues relative to what would be collected if organizational form was not flexible.

Several papers have examined the extent to which business organizational form responds to tax differentials. While evidence is conclusive that business organizational form responds to tax incentives, the magnitude of this effect and, ultimately, its impact on who bears the corporate income tax is uncertain. Mackie-Mason and Gordon (1997) and Goolsbee (1998) find relatively modest-sized effects on incorporation decisions based on time-series analysis; in contrast, relying

---

[19] While the incidence results based on the Gravelle and Kotlikoff models with endogenous organizational form are ambiguous when compared to the traditional formulations of the Harberger model, these models have much stronger predictions for the deadweight loss created by the tax. Both models predict that the deadweight loss of the corporate income tax could be much larger than predicted by the traditional Harberger model. The larger deadweight loss is important since a portion of the incidence of the tax comes from the deadweight loss and not just the tax revenue collected. Thus, when the deadweight loss is larger, the burdens of the tax can far outweigh the revenue collected.

on variation across states, Goolsbee (2003) finds a quite substantial effect of taxes on organizational form. Goolsbee (2003) also explores whether the choice of organizational form affects capital intensity and finds little evidence that capital intensity or wages are affected by the cross-state variation in corporate taxation. Clearly, organizational form choice is a dimension that can affect the revenues generated by the corporate tax; furthermore, as suggested by theoretical models, this margin may substantially increase the deadweight loss from corporate taxation. What remains less clear, especially given the evidence that suggests that labor demand may be similar for firms that switch organizational form due to tax incentives, is whether this margin has a substantial impact on the ultimate incidence of the corporate income tax?

V.   Conclusion

The incidence of the corporate income tax is an important issue for designing tax policy. Who bears the corporate income tax can affect overall conclusions about the progressivity of the tax system. Policy analysts have often made assumptions about how to allocate the corporate income tax in measuring the distribution of tax burdens. A common assumption, based on theoretical models of tax incidence, is that capital bears the burden of the corporate income tax. Recent empirical work using cross-country data on corporate taxes and wages suggests reconsidering this assumption; labor may actually bear a substantial burden from the corporate income tax. While this avenue for research seems promising, several statistical hurdles remain before definitive judgments can be drawn from this new research.

This empirical evidence is consistent with theoretical models of corporate tax incidence that assume that capital is mobile between countries and that foreign countries do not adjust their tax rates in response to a tax change by the domestic country. This theory assumes that capital is mobile between countries and that capital investment varies with tax policy. In the past, many economists would have argued against both of these propositions; however, recent empirical evidence on both capital mobility (in general and with respect to tax differentials) and the elasticity of investment with respect to the user cost of capital (including tax-induced changes in the user cost) support these assumptions. Thus, new evidence on capital mobility and investment corroborate the view that labor bears a substantial burden from the corporate income tax.

These arguments about capital mobility and investment focus on the main channel for the corporate tax affecting labor income is through changes in the capital stock. As Arulampalam, Devereux, and Maffini point out, these general equilibrium effects are not the only mechanism by which corporate tax liabilities can affect workers. Moving beyond the traditional models with competitive markets, labor can bear part of the corporate tax if wages are determined as a bargain over rents. This channel has received much less attention in terms of theoretical models and empirical work. Further exploration of this channel could be fruitful for determining the ultimate burden of the corporate income tax.

References

Arulampalam, Wiji, Michael P. Devereux, and Giorgia Maffini (2007). "The Incidence of Corporate Income Tax on Wages," Mimeo, University of Warwick, September.

Auerbach, Alan J. (2006). "Who Bears the Corporate Tax? A Review of What We Know," in James M. Poterba (ed.), *Tax Policy and the Economy*, vol. 20, Cambridge: MIT Press.

Auerbach, Alan J. and Kevin A. Hassett (2003). "On the Marginal Source of Investment Funds," *Journal of Public Economics*, 87:205-232.

Barthold, Thomas A., James R. Nunns, and Eric Toder (1995). "A Comparison of Distribution Methodologies," in David F. Bradford (ed.), *Distributional Analysis of Tax Policy*, Washington, DC: American Enterprise Institute Press.

Bernheim, B. Douglas (2002). "Taxation and Saving," in Alan J. Auerbach and Martin Feldstein (eds.), *Handbook of Public Economics*, vol. 3, Amsterdam: Elsevier.

Blanchard, Olivier and Francesco Giavazzi (2002). "Current Account Deficits in the Euro Area: The End of the Feldstein-Horioka Puzzle?" *Brookings Papers on Economic Activity*, 2002(2):147-186.

Bradford, David F. (1978). "Factor Prices May be Constant, but Factor Returns are Not," *Economics Letters*, 1(3):199-203.

Chirinko, Robert S. (2002). "Corporate Taxation, Capital Formation and the Substitution Elasticity between Labor and Capital," *National Tax Journal*, 55(2):339-355.

Coakley, Jerry, Ana-Maria Fuertes, and Fabio Spagnolo (2004). "Is the Feldstein-Horioka Puzzle History?" *Manchester School*, 72(5):569-590.

Cummins, Jason G., Kevin A. Hassett, and R. Glenn Hubbard (1994). "A Reconsideration of Investment Behavior Using Tax Reforms as Natural Experiments," *Brookings Papers on Economic Activity*, 1994(2):1-60.

Cummins, Jason G., Kevin A. Hassett, and R. Glenn Hubbard (1996). "Tax Reforms and Investment: A Cross-country Comparison," *Journal of Public Economics*, 62(1-2):237-273.

Davidson, Carl and Lawrence W. Martin (1985). "General Equilibrium Tax Incidence under Imperfect Competition: A Quantity-setting Supergame Analysis," *Journal of Political Economy*, 93(6):1212-1223.

Desai, Mihir A., C. Fritz Foley, and James R. Hines, Jr. (2004). "Foreign Direct Investment in a World of Multiple Taxes," *Journal of Public Economics*, 88(12):2727-2744.

Desai, Mihir A., C. Fritz Foley, and James R. Hines, Jr. (2005). "Foreign Direct Investment and the Domestic Capital Stock," *American Economic Review*, 95(2):33-38.

Dusansky, Richard (1972). "The Short-Run Shifting of the Corporation Income-Tax in the United States," *Oxford Economic Papers*, 24(3):357-371.

Edwards, Sebastian (1999). "How Effective are Capital Controls?" *Journal of Economic Perspectives*, 13(4):65-84.

Erkel-Rousse, Helene and Daniel Mirza (2002). "Import Price Elasticities: Reconsidering the Evidence," *Canadian Journal of Economics*, 35(2):282-306.

Feldstein, Martin S. and Charles Horioka (1980). "Domestic Savings and Capital Flows," *Economic Journal,* 90(2):314-329.

Feldstein, Martin S. and Marian Valliant Wrobel (1998). "Can State Taxes Redistribute Income?" *Journal of Public Economics*, 68(3):369-396.

Felix, R. Alison (2007), "Passing the Burden: Corporate Tax Incidence in Open Economies," Chapter 1, Ph.D. Dissertation, University of Michigan.

Frankel, Jeffrey A. (1992). "Measuring International Capital Mobility: A Review," *American Economic Review*, 82(2):197-202.

French Kenneth R. and James M. Poterba (1991). "Investor Diversification and International Equity Markets," *American Economic Review*, 81(2):222-226.

Fuest, Clemens, Bernd Huber, and Jack Mintz (2005). "Capital Mobility and Tax Competition," *Foundations and Trends in Microeconomics*, 1(1):1-62.

Goolsbee, Austan (1998). "Taxes, Organizational Form, and the Deadweight Loss of the Corporate Income Tax," *Journal of Public Economics*, 69(1):143-152.

Goolsbee, Austan (2003). "Investment Subsidies and Wages in Capital Goods Industries: To the Workers Go the Spoils?" *National Tax Journal*, 56(1, pt. 2):153-165.

Goolsbee, Austan (2004). "The Impact of the Corporate Income Tax: Evidence from State Organizational Form Data," *Journal of Public Economics*, 88(11):2283-2299.

Gordon, Robert J. (1967). "The Incidence of the Corporation Income Tax in U.S. Manufacturing, 1925-62," *American Economic Review*, 57(4):731-758.

Gordon, Roger H. (1992). "Can Capital Taxes Survive in an Open Economy?" *Journal of Finance*, 47(3):1159-1180.

Gravelle, Jane G. and Thomas L. Hungerford (2007). "Corporate Tax Reform: Issues for Congress," Congressional Research Service, Order Code RL34229, October 31, 2007.

Gravelle, Jane G. and Laurence J. Kotlikoff (1989). "The Incidence and Efficiency Costs of Corporate Taxation When Corporate and Noncorporate Firms Produce the Same Good," *Journal of Political Economy*, 97(4):749-780.

Gravelle, Jane G. and Laurence J. Kotlikoff (1993). "Corporate Tax Incidence and Inefficiency When Corporate and Noncorporate Goods are Close Substitutes," *Economic Inquiry*, 31(4):501-516.

Gravelle, Jane G. and Kent A. Smetters (2006). "Does the Open Economy Assumption Really Mean That Labor Bears the Burden of a Capital Income Tax?" *Advances in Economic Analysis & Policy*, 6(1): Article 3.

Harberger, Arnold C. (1962). "The Incidence of the Corporation Income Tax," *Journal of Political Economy*, 70(3):215-240.

Harberger, Arnold C. (1995). "The ABC's of Corporate Tax Incidence: Insights into the Open Economy Case," in *Tax Policy and Economic Growth*, Washington, DC: American Council for Capital Formation.

Harberger, Arnold C. (2006). "Corporation Tax Incidence: Reflections on What is Known, Unknown and Unknowable," in John W. Diamond and George R. Zodrow (eds.), *Fundamental Tax Reform: Issues, Choices, and Implications*, Cambridge: MIT Press, forthcoming.

Hassett, Kevin A. and R. Glenn Hubbard (2002). "Tax Policy and Business Investment," in Alan J. Auerbach and Martin Feldstein (eds.), *Handbook of Public Economics*, vol. 3, Amsterdam: Elsevier.

Hassett, Kevin A. and Aparna Mathur (2006). "Taxes and Wages," American Enterprise Insitute for Public Policy Research Working Paper #128, June.

Kotlikoff, Laurence and Lawrence Summers (1987). "Tax Incidence in a Life Cycle Model with Variable Labor Supply," *Quarterly Journal of Economics*, 93(4):705-718.

Krzyzaniak, Marian and Richard A. Musgrave (1963). *The Shifting of the Corporation Income Tax*, Baltimore, MD: Johns Hopkins University Press.

Mackie-Mason, Jeffrey K. and Roger H. Gordon (1997). "How Much Do Taxes Discourage Incorporation?" *Journal of Finance*, 52(2):477-505.

Melvin, James R. (1982). "The Corporate Income Tax in an Open Economy," *Journal of Public Economics*, 17(3):393-403.

Mulligan, Casey B. (2002). "Capital Tax Incidence: First Impressions from the Time Series," National Bureau of Economic Research Working Paper No. 9374, Cambridge, MA, December.

Mulligan, Casey B. (2003). "Capital Tax Incidence: Fisherian Impressions from the Time Series," National Bureau of Economic Research Working Paper No. 9916, Cambridge, MA, August.

Mulligan, Casey B. (2004). "What Do Aggregate Consumption Euler Equations Say about the Capital-Income Tax Burden?" *American Economic Review*, 94(2):166-170.

Mutti, John and Harry Grubert (1985). "The Taxation of Capital Income in an Open Economy: the Importance of Resident-Nonresident Tax Treatment," *Journal of Public Economics*, 27(3):291-309.

Oakland, William (1972). "Corporation Earnings and Tax Shifting in U.S. Manufacturing, 1930-68," *Review of Economics and Statistics*, 54(3):235-244.

Obstfeld, Maurice (1995). "International Capital Mobility in the 1990s," in Peter B. Kenen (ed.), *Understanding Interdependence: The Macroeconomics of the Open Economy*, Princeton: Princeton University Press.

Randolph, William C. (2006). "International Burdens of the Corporate Income Tax," Congressional Budget Office Working Paper Series 2006-09, Washington DC.

Sebold, Frederick D. (1979). "The Short-Run Shifting of the Corporation Income Tax: A Simultaneous Equation Approach," *Review of Economics and Statistics*, 61(3):401-409.

Stiglitz, Joseph E. (1973). "Taxation, Corporate Financial Policy and the Cost of Capital," *Journal of Public Economics*, 2(1):1-34.

Tesar, Linda L. and Ingrid M. Werner (1995). "Home Bias and High Turnover," *Journal of International Money and Finance*, 14(4):467-492.